GOD'S PLAN
FOR YOUR LIFE

GOD'S PLAN FOR YOUR LIFE

DR. HENRY WOLMARANS

NAVIGATOR BOOKS
SAN DIEGO, CALIFORNIA

GOD'S PLAN FOR YOUR LIFE

Copyright © 2013 by Henry Wolmarans

Navigator Books

www.navigator-books.com

ISBN-13: 978-0-9890026-5-3

Printed in the United States of America

PREFACE

I have a few very challenging questions for you before you start this book. While you might have a different perspective after reading the book, for right now would you try to answer these questions as honestly as you can?

1. **If someone had to ask you what God's plan for your life was, what would you say?**

2. **Do you think you will go to heaven when you die?**

3. **Suppose you did die, and you wanted to go to heaven; why do you think God should let you in? Is there something you have done that would merit entrance to heaven?**

4. **Do you think that before you could go to heaven, God would expect you to change anything about the way you live right now?**

Are you perhaps at a crossroads in your spiritual life?

Reading this book may be the most important step you ever take to discover GOD'S PLAN FOR YOU.

TABLE OF CONTENTS

CHAPTER ONE

Let's start at the beginning

In the beginning when God made man, He made him perfect. He wanted man to be His friend.

But, God did NOT make a robot. He gave him a powerful gift that men and women were supposed to use wisely: the gift of choice, a free will. Man used this powerful gift adversely and plunged the entire world into a cursed state separated from God's provision. God judged this action as sin and penalized it with the death sentence. Separated from God, man died spiritually instantly but he also began to age and die physically.

This death sentence was extremely serious because it affected the entire human race forever, since everyone born after this first man Adam would be born subject to this curse and under the punishment of death. As a result of Adam's action his sin was passed onto his children and their children; therefore in Adam **ALL** have sinned.

Most people do not consider themselves to be "sinners" because they think that sin refers to murder, violence, robbery, rape and those things that are especially wicked. However doing these things doesn't make us a sinner. It is because we are a sinner that we do these things. It is our nature to sin just as it is the nature of a lemon tree to produce lemons.

If we have a tender conscience, we are aware that we are producing lemons, but the harder we try to stop such behavior the worse we seem to get. We feel dirty as if the sin is an ugly blot on a clean page. Sin is incredibly destructive. It ruins people's character, destroys relationships and separates them from God.

Is there a solution to this dilemma? Is there a way out from this death sentence? What can be done to rectify the situation?

There is good news and there is bad news. First the bad news: You cannot save yourself, just as a drowning man cannot pull himself out of the water by his hair. Making New Year's resolutions to change or to be better is only a temporary fix. Doing good deeds for others will make us feel better but will never remove the bad ones from our past or the consequences arising from those poor decisions. Here is the good news.

God has a solution to our problem.

God has set a plan in motion to save us. Unfortunately His plan doesn't work for everyone even though it's made available to everyone. Let me explain, if you want it you can have it. But you must receive it on God's terms without any negotiation or bargaining. Making a case to justify ourselves—that we are not as bad as so and so—will not open the door for God's plan to work in our life. We must humbly accept God's forgiveness provided in His redemption plan and understand that Only His plan will work. No amount of ingenuity on your part can clear you of your sin, guilt, or the curse of eternal death.

God's answer is the cross of His Son, where He proved and demonstrated His love for us.

Be quite clear about this: hell is a grim and dreadful reality for all who reject Jesus Christ in this life. Jesus Christ is God's plan of salvation for all mankind, every human being irrespective of race, color, ethnic group or religion must come to The Father through Jesus and call on His name in order to be saved. There is no other name given to man by God for us to be saved by or through.

What are you going to do about it?

Step 1: Believe in Jesus with all your heart

Belief in Christ is the same sort of belief we exercise when we jump out of an airplane and trust a parachute to carry us safely to the ground. It's the kind of faith we use when we climb aboard an airplane and entrust our lives to a pilot whom we have never seen, nor tested his ability to fly us safely to our destination. Some might refer to this as blind faith but really it is enlightened faith because Jesus is the light of the world and the only way to God. Once you've believed this, you have "seen the light".

You need to believe that Jesus is The Son of The Living God and that He paid with His life for you to be saved from eternal punishment.

Step 2: Acknowledge and confess.

Acknowledge and confess that you are a sinner in the sight of God. Be deeply sorry for your sin. Hate it and be willing to turn from every thought, word, action and habit that you know is wrong and displeasing to God.

Step 3: Make the decision to follow Jesus.

Make a decision to be a dedicated follower Jesus. This means to turn away from evil deeds and wrong things and cultivate a new lifestyle that corresponds to the Bible's description of a Christian. Crown Jesus as your Lord and Savior.

> *"...that if you confess with your mouth the Lord Jesus and believe in your heart that God has raised Him from the dead, you will be saved. For with the heart one believes unto righteousness, and with the mouth confession is made unto salvation."*
> —Romans 10:9, 10 NKJ

Notice that salvation is a result of **two things;** the first believing in your heart that God raised Jesus from the dead. Then, saying with your mouth "Jesus you are my Lord."

You are not required to confess every sin you ever committed but only repent for not believing that Jesus is the Christ; the Son of the Living God.

Through this simple prayer we call the prayer of salvation you invite the Spirit of Jesus to come into your heart, the very center of your being and you proclaim that Jesus is now your Lord.

> *"Yet to all who received him, to those who believed in his name, he gave the right to become children of God"*
> —John 1:12 NIV

Notice only those who believe on the Name of Jesus and receive Him as their savior are given the right or authority to call themselves Children of God. I know how that sounds because we are raised to believe that all humans are automatically considered children of God but that's not what the Bible teaches.

I hope you can now see why God's salvation plan doesn't work for everyone. It's not because God doesn't love them or because they are so wicked but rather because they must believe on Jesus with their whole heart.

God's plan for you is salvation.

It is not the will of God that anyone be lost eternally. He has made a plan whereby ALL who call on the name of Jesus will be saved. We must acknowledge that we have sinned and thereby evoked the judgment that justice demands - "death."However, if we receive Jesus Christ as our Lord and Savior, our sin is forgiven and we become children of God. God's grace that is His unmerited, unearned favor is available to you, right now.

Do you desire to take the first step in receiving God's plan for your life? *Then make the decision to pray this prayer out loud.* Be sincere and determined to go all the way with God.

"I believe that Jesus Christ is the Son of God; that He came to earth in the flesh and died on the cross, taking my sin upon Himself. I believe that God the Father raised Jesus from the dead. I repent for my sin and for not believing in Jesus but I now receive Jesus as my Lord and Savior. Thank you Father for saving me and forgiving me in Jesus' name, amen."

Now say this: *"I know that I am now a child of God and a born-again Christian, that my name has been written in God's book of life. I have been saved by receiving God's free gift. I am determined to do the Word faithfully by trusting the Holy Spirit to lead me."*

I boldly proclaim on the authority of the infallible Scriptures, that you are now born of God, saved from the penalty of your sins, declared righteous, have become a new creature in Christ and have the right to be called a CHILD OF GOD.

NOTES

_____

_____

_____

_____

_____

_____

_____

_____

_____

_____

_____

_____

_____

_____

_____

_____

_____

_____

_____

_____

_____

_____

_____

CHAPTER TWO

Understanding what has happened to you

You are saved.

You have taken the most important step in your entire life: accepting Jesus as your Savior. This is the beginning of God's plan for you.

> *"For it is by grace you have been saved, through faith—and this not from yourselves, it is the gift of God— not by works, so that no one can boast."*
> —Ephesians 2:8, 9 NIV

Salvation and redemption are the most important themes of the entire Bible. The name Jesus means Savior. The very purpose Jesus came to earth was to **SAVE** lost mankind from the punishment due them because of sin.

Never forget that **salvation cannot be earned,** it can only be received by faith as a gift. This is one reason why the believer is always full of thanksgiving, gratitude or praise. We will explore grace more fully in a later chapter.

Do not be afraid of the word "saved." It is a basic Bible term. The believer, who says, "I am saved," is neither a hopeful thinker nor a proud, boastful or irreverent person. He or she is simply one who believes that God means what He says.

> *"Everyone who calls on the name of the Lord will be saved"*
> —Romans 10:13 NIV

We are saved through faith, by putting our trust in the accomplishment of Christ's death on the cross, which paid for our sins. We are not saved by anything we do. The Christian faith, it has been said, is one of four letters — D.O.N.E all other religions are religions of two letters — D.O.

Salvation is available because of God's unearned and undeserved favor or grace. We are simply asked to believe in what Jesus accomplished through His death and resurrection, the great act of Redemption. I cannot add to it I simply receive it by faith and thank God for it.

You have been born again.

In John Chapter 3, we read about Nicodemus, a very sincere man and a well-respected leader of the Jews. He asked Jesus what he needed to do to be saved. Even though Nicodemus was apparently a good man, Jesus said he needed to be born again. Jesus made it clear that not only the really wicked, but men like Nicodemus also needed the 'new birth.' It is through receiving Jesus that you become a child of God. This experience of being born into God's family has nothing to do with physical birth. It is the rebirth of the human spirit. *If you prayed the prayer with me in the beginning of this book then you have had the spiritual experience of being born again.*

Realize that you are at the beginning of a new life and be willing to become childlike with simple sincerity so that you may grow in your faith. The safest and quickest way to grow is to have spiritual mentors who love you and who are concerned for your spiritual wellbeing. **You cannot afford to be a lone ranger; this independent or rebellious attitude will open the door to our enemy the devil to mislead you.** You must, because of your recent rebirth, realize your dependence on others to instruct, mature and train you.

You are now a Christian.

You are **not** a CHRISTIAN because:

- You were brought up in a Christian home
- Your mother always prayed for you and she went to Church
- You believe in doing good and helping others
- You have been baptized and confirmed
- You believe in God
- You go to Church

As good as these things may be, they DON'T qualify you as a Christian. You are a child of God because you have decided to believe and trust in Jesus. When you did, you had a true conversion, and have been born again and saved.

You should be absolutely confident that you will go to heaven when you die and that God will let you in, not because of what you have done but because of your faith in what Jesus has done.

You should be absolutely sure of your salvation.

"Anyone who believes in the Son of God has this testimony in his heart. Anyone who does not believe God, has made him out to be a liar, because he has not believed the testimony God has given about his Son. And this is the testimony: God has given us eternal life, and this life is in his Son. He who has the Son has life; he who does not have the Son of God does not have life. I write these things to you who believe in the name of the Son of God so that you may KNOW that you have eternal life."
—1 John 5:10-13 NIV

The Bible does not use the word "HOPE," it specifically states "KNOW." All the scriptures studied thus far have been chosen to ground you in your salvation and to show you that it is not presumptuous to believe God means what He says. If you believe the written Word, it will create great confidence, assurance and peace. Doubting this implies that God is a liar. We must accept His Word as final authority! I like this statement "God said it; that settles it" You should "KNOW" that you have eternal life." That's the reason the Bible was written.

Some of your friends will think you are a religious nut, even lacking humility because you claim that you know you are "saved" and that "you are sure you will go to heaven." Make it clear to them that you are just taking God at His Word. God has clearly stated that He gives to us eternal life, and that this life is in Christ. If we have accepted Christ we have eternal life; if we have not accepted Christ we do not have life. It is as simple as that.

Do not let anyone ever rob you of this assurance of salvation. You are Christ's and He is yours forevermore. He said "I will never leave you, nor forsake you" and "no one will be able to pluck you out of My hand". However, God will not exercise power over your will. If you choose to walk away from serving Jesus, He will reach out in love to you but will never force you to go to heaven against your will.

You have received "The Gift of Righteousness."

Remember that you received salvation as a gift and you did it by faith. Well, when you were saved you also received another gift that you were not aware of. It is called the gift of righteousness.

> *"For if, by the trespass of the one man, death reigned through that one man, how much more will those who receive God's abundant provision of grace and of the gift of righteousness reign in life through the one man, Jesus Christ."*
> —Romans 5:17 NIV

Righteousness means to be in right standing with God, which means that God is not hostile toward you anymore and there are no sins blocking your relationship with Him.

NOTES

_____

_____

_____

_____

_____

_____

_____

_____

_____

_____

_____

_____

_____

_____

_____

_____

_____

_____

_____

_____

_____

_____

_____

_____

_____

CHAPTER THREE

What should I do next?

The same question was asked of Peter, one of the original twelve Apostles, and he replied as follows:

> *"Peter replied, 'Repent and be baptized, every one of you, in the name of Jesus Christ for the forgiveness of your sins. And you will receive the gift of the Holy Spirit.'"*
> —Acts 2:38 NIV

The next step is to be baptized in water.

Before you take this important step, you should understand what baptism signifies. Baptism is a burial service of the past lifestyle and a public acknowledgement that you have accepted Jesus Christ as your Lord and Savior, vowing to live like a Christian.

> *"Therefore go and make disciples of all nations, baptizing them in the name of the Father and of the Son and of the Holy Spirit, 20 and teaching them to obey everything I have commanded you."*
> —Matthew 28:19 NIV

> *"He who believes and is baptized will be saved."*
> —Mark 16:16 NIV

Baptism is a public acknowledgement of **a new ruling power in your life** showing that a change of government has taken place. Jesus is not only your Savior but He is your LORD and the Word of God has final authority in your life.

Christian baptism demonstrates the believer's identification with Christ's death, burial and resurrection.

> *"Or don't you know that all of us who were baptized into Christ Jesus were baptized into his death? We were therefore buried with him through baptism into death in order that, just as Christ was raised from the dead through the glory of the Father, we too may live a new life. If we have been united with him like this in his death, we will certainly also be united with him in his resurrection."*
—Romans 6:3 NIV

Many of us have seen infant baptisms and were perhaps baptized that way ourselves; unfortunately sprinkling of babies cannot be found anywhere in the Bible. The reason should be obvious; babies are too immature to repent of their sins, which is the only requirement before baptism can take place.

Based on these references it is obvious that baptism by **total immersion** is the only scriptural way of being baptized.

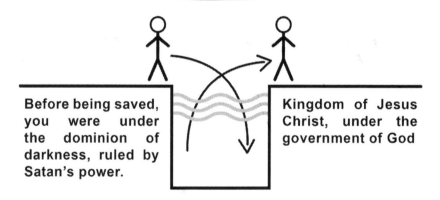

Before being saved, you were under the dominion of darkness, ruled by Satan's power.

Kingdom of Jesus Christ, under the government of God

Grave (Baptism Symbolic of Salvation)

NOTES

CHAPTER FOUR

God's Gift of the Holy Spirit

When Peter was asked "what to do following repentance" remember his reply? He said: *"Repent and be baptized, every one of you, in the name of Jesus Christ for the forgiveness of your sins.* **And you will receive the gift of the Holy Spirit."** —Acts 2:38 NIV

God now wants to give you the Gift of the Holy Spirit.

A gift is neither earned nor deserved. A gift is received with thanks. The gift of the Holy Spirit is only available to believers, those folks who have repented and received Jesus as lord. You therefore qualify. Many Christians have not received the gift of the Holy Spirit as a second experience after salvation simply because they didn't know the gift was available. Others unfortunately are told or taught that they received the Holy Spirit when they got saved. Actually everyone receives the Spirit of Christ at conversion but the fullness or baptism of the Holy Spirit with the gift of tongues can only be received once you're saved.

Why is it important to receive the indwelling third person of the Godhead? We know God is with us all the time anyway but the presence of the Holy Spirit was vital for Jesus to fulfill His ministry and so important that He decided to ask the Father for us to have Him in us.

Among the many vitally important reasons for receiving the fullness of the Holy Spirit is that one receives the gift of praying in an unknown, angelic tongue; a supernatural prayer language.

If you have ever desired to pray the perfect will of God, then this is the answer to that desire. It doesn't matter how young you are, or how mature you are as a Christian; you can pray the perfect will of God immediately after receiving the Holy Spirit by praying in your new heavenly prayer language.

*"In the same way, the Spirit helps us in our weakness. We do not know what we ought to pray for, but the Spirit himself intercedes for us with groans that words cannot express. And he who searches our hearts knows the mind of the Spirit, **because the Spirit intercedes for the saints in accordance with God's will.**"*
—Romans 8:26 NIV

This important verse teaches us about our new prayer language and how the Holy Spirit can pray through us for the needs of other Christians that may even be unknown to us.

When praying by the Spirit we talk to God in a supernatural way and He understands what we are saying even if we don't.

"For anyone who speaks in a tongue does not speak to men but to God. Indeed, no one understands him; he utters mysteries with his spirit."
—1 Corinthians 14:2 NIV

Through this method of praying we also build up our spirit man; it's like feeding him a good steak.

"But you, beloved, build yourselves up [founded] on your most holy faith [make progress, rise like an edifice higher and higher], praying in the Holy Spirit."
—Jude 1:20 Amp

Tongues is a supernatural sign available to all.

"And it happened, while Apollos was at Corinth, that Paul, having passed through the upper regions, came to Ephesus. And finding some disciples he said to them, 'Did you receive the Holy Spirit when you believed?' and they said to him, 'We have not so much as heard whether there is a Holy Spirit.' And when Paul had laid hands on them, the Holy Spirit came upon them, and they spoke with tongues and prophesied."
—Acts 19:1, 2, 6 NKJ

Notice that these believers were considered disciples or followers of Jesus, however they did not receive the Holy Spirit at their conversion. They only received the Holy Spirit when Paul laid his hands on them.

It is clearly seen from the above scripture that the initial sign of having received the Holy Spirit is the God-given, supernatural gift of being able to speak in other tongues. This occurred on the day of Pentecost when the Holy Spirit was first poured out upon the earth.

"And they were all filled with the Holy Spirit and BEGAN to speak with other tongues, as the Spirit gave them utterance."
—Acts 2:4 NKJ

God wants ALL believers to receive the Holy Spirit and speak in other tongues.

"I wish you ALL spoke with tongues"
—1 Corinthians 14:5 NKJ

"I thank my God I speak with tongues more than you all"
—1 Corinthians 14:18 NKJ

Paul the Apostle was a tongue talker, as were all the New Testament writers including Mary the mother of Jesus. In fact God is emphatic that no one should disallow speaking in tongues.

"DO NOT FORBID to speak with tongues."
—1 Corinthians 14:39 NKJ

Speaking in tongues is also referred to as your heavenly prayer language or praying in the Spirit.

God's Gift of Power

Being born-again gets you ready to live in heaven, but receiving the Holy Spirit gives you the power to live on earth as a Christian.

"But you shall receive POWER when the Holy Spirit has come upon you"
—Acts 1:8 NKJ

Go on and fulfill God's plan for your life. Ask God for the Holy Spirit and your heavenly prayer language. It is a gift received purely by faith and not as a reward for good works.

How to Receive the Holy Spirit

Generally Christians who have as yet not received the Holy Spirit with the evidence of speaking in other tongues have one or more of the following hurdles to overcome:

They may think they are not ready to receive. However, there is only one condition mentioned in the Bible that you need to meet before you are ready to receive the Holy Spirit: Repent and be born again.

Others may feel they don't deserve the Holy Spirit. But the Holy Spirit is a gift. You can never deserve Him, earn Him or receive Him as a reward. The only qualification required is salvation.

Still others believe "God will fill them with the Holy Spirit when He wants to." He has already given the Holy Spirit to us. We must simply receive Him. Don't beg God, but just say thank you for the gift of the Holy Spirit.

Many don't realize that they must do the speaking, using their vocal cords. The Holy Spirit does not make the sounds. He gives you the ability to speak. *"...when the Holy Spirit came on them 'THEY SPOKE'"* —Acts 19:6

NOTES

CHAPTER FIVE

It is God's plan for you to be a worshiper

Praise and worship is a vital part of every true believer's LIFESTYLE. Not only in Church, but also and more importantly in our private devotions. In fact, one's heart is often continuously full of thankfulness and praise to God. This joy can and should be expressed outwardly by singing, clapping and even dancing.

> *"But the hour is coming, and now is, when the true worshippers will worship the Father in spirit and truth; for the Father is seeking such to worship Him. God is Spirit, and those who worship Him MUST worship in spirit and truth."*
> —John 4:23,24 NKJ

How do we worship God?

We bow down and kneel.

> *"O come, let us worship and BOW DOWN; let us KNEEL before the Lord our Maker."*
> —Psalm 95:6 NKJ

We stand and sing, giving audible praise to God.

> *"After these things I looked, and behold, a great multitude which no one could number, of all nations, tribes, peoples, and tongues, STANDING before the throne and before the Lamb, clothed with white robes, with palm branches in their hands, and crying out with a LOUD VOICE, saying, 'Salvation belongs to our God who sits on*

19

the throne and to the Lamb!'"
—Revelation 7:9, 10

"Therefore by Him let us continually offer the sacrifice of praise to God, that is, the FRUIT OF OUR LIPS, giving thanks to His name."
—Hebrews 13:15

We clap our hands and shout in victory.

"Oh, CLAP YOUR HANDS, all you peoples! SHOUT to God with a voice of triumph!"
—Psalm 47:1

We lift our hands in prayer and praise of God.

"Thus I will bless you while I live; I will LIFT up my hands in your name."
—Psalm 63:4

"LIFT up your hands in the sanctuary, and bless the Lord."
—Psalm 134:2

We dance as a form of praise to the Lord.

"Praise the Lord! Sing to the Lord a new song, and His praise in the congregation of saints. Let Israel rejoice in their Maker; Let the children of Zion be joyful in their King. Let them praise His name with the DANCE; Let them sing praises to Him with the timbrel and harp."
—Psalm 149:1-3

"Praise Him with the timbrel and DANCE"
—Psalm 150:4

"Then David DANCED before the Lord with all his might."
—2 Samuel 6:14

We sing in tongues, and in English.

"For if I pray in a tongue, my SPIRIT PRAYS, but my understanding is unfruitful. What is the result then? I will pray with the spirit, and I will also pray with the understanding. I will SING WITH THE SPIRIT, and I will also sing with the understanding."
—1 Corinthians 14:14-15

Musical instruments are used as part of the worship service.

"Praise Him with the sound of the trumpet; Praise Him with the lute and harp! Praise Him with the timbrel and dance; Praise Him with stringed instruments and flutes! Praise Him with loud cymbals, and praise Him with clashing cymbals!"
—Psalm 150:3-5

NOTES

CHAPTER SIX

God's goal for your life

God's ultimate goal for you is not heaven! It is for you to be conformed to the image of Jesus.

> *"For whom he did foreknow, he also did predestinate to be conformed to the image of his Son, that he might be the firstborn among many brethren."*
> —Romans 8:29 NKJ

This little sketch below illustrates the fall of man in Adam to a state of being dead in sin, God's plan to bring man back into right standing with Himself, and finally, His goal for man, as man lives out his Christian life, which is being conformed to the image of Jesus Christ.

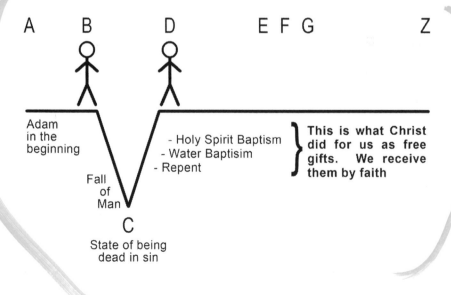

Points D to Z represent the road you walk as a Christian. On this road God works **IN** and **THROUGH** you. Not only does He expect you to change certain habits, attitudes and characteristics, but also He desires for you to take on the **character of His son Jesus Christ.**

The character of Jesus is clearly seen in

"The fruit of the Spirit is love, joy, peace, longsuffering, kindness, goodness, faithfulness, gentleness and self-control."
—Galatians 5:22, 23 NKJ

Allow the Holy Spirit to work in your life to produce these fruits. This won't always be painless, but I can assure you that it will never be without reward.

You have become a citizen of the Kingdom of God

As you travel the road of life, from point C to Z, you will learn to walk with Jesus in a very special relationship. This relationship is like being **yoked together** with Him in such a way that He gently guides your life.

Jesus said *"Come to Me, all you who labor and are heavy laden, and I will give you rest. Take My yoke upon you and learn from Me, for I am gentle and lowly in heart, and you will find rest for your souls. For My yoke is easy and My burden is light."* —Matthew 11:28-30 NKJ

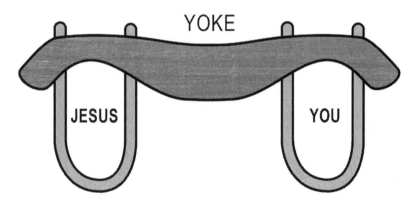

One needs to understand that a yoke is a **symbol of the Kingdom of God** that represents the government of Jesus Christ. You must also understand the need to put your life into this yoke, however light or easy, and to be yoked with Jesus Christ in such a way that the yoke dictates your way of life.

As a citizen of the Kingdom of God we willingly submit to Jesus as our Lord and King. Remember God's goal is to develop Christ in you. When we finally stand before God He will not judge us by our works for Him but He will judge to what degree we have become like Jesus.

NOTES

CHAPTER SEVEN

God's plan is your spiritual growth

Getting you started in the Bible

Your spiritual growth will be directly proportionate to the amount of time you give to reading, studying and meditating in the scriptures. We are told to *"desire the pure milk of the Word as new born babes that we may grow."* —1 Peter 2:1-3

The Bible is no ordinary book! It is actually like a whole library of books bound together under one cover, written down by many human vessels that were inspired and guided by the Holy Spirit (2 Peter 1:21).

In a sense, you could even say that the Bible is like a special series of letters, written personally to you by God... to inspire you, teach you, guide you, show you where you are wrong, and give you good ideas (2 Timothy 3:16).

The question for you now is, where to begin? Some of the books of the Bible were written with the purpose of helping people who have just begun to follow Jesus. The best of these is the *Gospel of John*. It gives us the clearest understanding of who Jesus Christ is. So begin reading the *Gospel of John*, even if you have read the Bible before. It will help you most now.

Set yourself a goal to read at least a chapter a day.

It won't take long. The important thing is to find a time when you can give your undivided attention to the reading and study of God's Word. Set this time aside as a daily appointment with the Lord to hear Him speak to you in His Word. Choose a definite time and stick to it, then your Bible reading will be accomplished! But if you just wait until you "feel like it", the devil will make sure you never "feel like it." CHOOSE YOUR TIME NOW.

The devil starts getting nervous when he sees you reading the Bible and thinking about what it says, the reason being that when you read the Bible:

a) You learn what God wants you to do

b) God Himself speaks to you in the words of the Bible

c) You are encouraged, inspired and strengthened

d) You know when you are wrong and need to make adjustments

e) You learn many powerful truths like how to be healed, how to prosper financially, how to increase your faith, etc.

Don't just read the Bible like a magazine, study it! Underline the parts you particularly like, so that you can find them again. Put Question Marks (???) next to anything you find hard to understand and ask your Pastor what it means. Memorize any verses that are really meaningful and helpful to you. Use colors to mark different themes such as **Love**, **Healing**, **Faith**, and **Holy Spirit**.

Now, start doing what you read! Someone once said "Don't worry about the things in the Bible you don't understand. Rather worry about the things you DO understand and are not doing." Christianity is not so much what you have stopped doing but what you have STARTED doing.

Applying God's Word

It is vital that you realize the importance of studying and applying God's Word in every area of your life, since this is the only way you will have your needs met.

*"But be **doers** of the word, and not hearers only, deceiving yourselves"*
—James 1:22

One scripture believed and applied is worth more than reading the entire Bible. Many people have the wrong idea of why the Bible has been given to us. Many have no idea at all! D.L. Moody, a world famous evangelist and Bible teacher said, "The Word of God was given mainly to guide our steps, not to increase our knowledge."

How do you, in a practical way, go about applying the Word in your life? Applying the Word of God means to take a verse or portion of scripture that speaks to your heart, meditate on it, and take practical steps to make it a living, vital part of your daily life.

Here are five simple steps to take when applying a verse to your life - Ask yourself:

#1 What does this passage say to me?

#2 Where am I falling short? (missing it)

#3 Think of specific examples concerning #1 and #2

#4 What am I going to do about it?

#5 Do it!

The Bible is not a theoretical or a historical book, but a very practical up-to-date manual for living a fulfilled life. Promise God that you will do whatever you read in the Bible, and you are on your way to victory!

Let me give you a hand to grow

To help you remember the five things you will need to do to get the Word into you in a practical way is illustrated by-a hand holding the Bible where each finger represents a learning action.

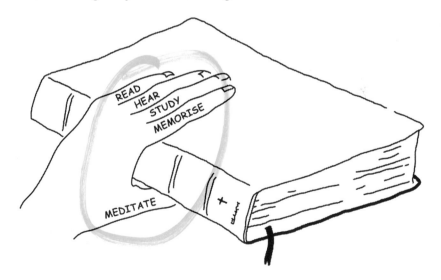

Read the Word

Let's start with the need to read the Word: Reading the Word is the little finger of the hand.

A daily reading of the Bible is very important as it gives the Holy Spirit a chance to teach us, minister to us, and give us instruction for that day. It allows the Lord an opportunity to change our lives so that our lives line up with what He expects. Until you develop a daily habit of reading the Bible you will always remain a baby Christian, and always be dependent on someone else to feed you.

"Blessed (happy, to be envied) is the man who READS ALOUD (in the assemblies) the Word of this prophecy; and blessed (happy, to be envied) are those who HEAR (IT READ) and who keep themselves true to the things which are written in it - heeding them and laying them to heart - for the time (for them to be fulfilled) is near."
—Revelation 1:3 Amp

Notice it says that you are blessed if you READ the scripture ALOUD! It benefits you to read aloud because then you HEAR the Word and there is something special that happens when you hear the Word.

Hear the Word

Hearing the Word is the ring finger.

"So then faith comes by hearing, and hearing by the Word of God."
Romans 10:17

The Bible says that without faith it is impossible to please God and that we are **to walk, stand, and live, by faith**. So it is most important that we hear the Word so that we can obtain faith.

There are a number of ways in which you can hear the Word:

a) You can read the Bible aloud to yourself.

b) You can download from the internet audio recordings of messages preached by anointed speakers.

c) You will hear the Word on Sundays at the Church and at the small group/cell meetings during the week.

d) There are also special courses you can take to learn special skills.

e) You can also buy the New Testament or the Old Testament on tape/cd/dvd/mp3 and listen to that in your car or during your quiet time.

Hearing the Word should be a daily thing you do as this feeds your spirit man with spiritual food which it needs in order to grow and stay alive.

Study the Word

Studying the Word is the middle finger of the hand.

*"Be **diligent** to present yourself approved to God, a worker who does not need to be ashamed, rightly dividing the word of truth."*
—2 Timothy 2:15

God sees you as a workman and says in this verse that you should be diligent or STUDY TO BE APPROVED BY HIM. An approved workman correctly understands the Word and therefore will not be deceived or misled.

"These were more fair-minded than those in Thessalonica, in that they received the word with all readiness, and SEARCHED the scriptures daily to find out whether these things were so."
—Acts 17:11

Notice that these Jewish Christians were eager to hear the Word and received it with an open mind. They then did something more with the Scriptures on a daily basis. What was it they did? They **searched** the Scriptures!

Studying the scriptures and searching the Word every day leads you into personal discoveries of God's truths. This experience is so beautiful and satisfying that nothing should take its place. You will actually feel yourself grow spiritually as you discover new things about God and who you are in Christ.

Memorize the Word

Memorizing the Word is the index finger. It's time for you as a Christian to now begin memorizing a NEW scripture every week. Once you've memorized the Word you can recall it at will. This will be necessary as you resist Satan, witness to others, and pray or confess a promise you that are believing for.

> *"Your word I have **hidden** in my heart, that I might not sin against You."*
> —Psalm 119:11

Your heart is the very center of your being and life. The Word should be hidden in the very core of your life, your innermost part. That's how God wants you to remember His Word so that you can never forget it.

> *"I will **not forget** your Word"*
> —Psalm 119:16

To memorize the Word will take diligent effort. Many people say, "Oh I have such a poor memory, I'll never be able to remember the Bible." But no one has a poor memory; you can't forget something once you have "put it into your memory." Take one verse that really means something to you from a Bible that's easy to read. Start by writing it down, then repeat the first word, then the first phrase, then the first sentence aloud to yourself a few times. Once you have a little confidence, try to use that verse three times during that week while talking to others. Once you have used it three times, it will be yours.

As a help, write the verse down on a small piece of cardboard and carry it with you in your pocket or handbag, and when you have a spare moment, glance over it. Think how surprised your friends and relatives will be when they hear you quoting the Bible!

Now, try to remember the verse's reference so that you can find it in the Bible.

Meditating on the Word

This is the thumb of the hand helping you to grow. It is really the combination of all the other growth actions.

> *"I will meditate on Your precepts, and contemplate on Your ways."*
> —Psalm 119:15

Meditation means to ponder, think about, whisper to yourself or talk to yourself about something. I'm sure you have worried about a problem before, well that's exactly what meditation is, but in the negative sense.

In order to think deeply about the promises of God, it is first necessary to read, hear, study and memorize the scriptures. The result will be that you will prosper and be successful, since you will have divine wisdom.

"This Book of the Law shall not depart from your mouth, but you shall meditate in it day and night, that you may observe to do according to all that is written in it. For then you will make your way prosperous and then you will have good success."
—Joshua 1:8

NOTES

Chapter Eight

God wants to talk to you

God's will is the privilege of a powerful prayer life.

As we read our Bibles every day to hear what God is saying to us, just so, we should set a particular time aside each day at least 15 minutes to talk to God. Choose a time that you will pray every day; DO IT NOW.

Prayer is really communicating with God.

The Bible says, "pray without ceasing". God keeps no office hours and is always available to hear us. Unfortunately many Christians have neglected this privilege and taken it so for granted that they only use it when in desperate need. This is abusing your privilege! Ensure you develop a good habit of talking to God frequently.

How do I pray? is a question all Christians ask. Remember God is now your Heavenly Father. Jesus taught US to pray "OUR FATHER" and the true meaning of that in today's language would be "OUR DAD." Because of this closeness and love, your prayers should not be stiff or formal.

Don't use long words or religious phrases; simply talk to God as you would to a close friend.

> *"This is the confidence we have in approaching God: that if we ask anything according to his will, he hears us. And if we know that he hears us — whatever we ask — we know that we have what we asked of him."*
> —1 John 5:14 NIV

Here are a few simple steps to follow that will help you pray correctly:

First, simply praise God. That means tell Him how much you love and appreciate Him.

Always pray directly to the Father.

Ask forgiveness for any things you have done wrong. Be specific; name it (privately).

Be clear about what you want.

Be sure your desires are scriptural.

Pray out loud with confidence.

Ask in Jesus' Name.

Thank God for hearing and answering you.

You have the privilege of being able to pray powerful prayers

A committed believer is a righteous person because he remains in living, vital fellowship with God. He abides in the Word and therefore has a powerful prayer life. God answers him when he prays.

> *"The earnest prayer of a righteous person has great power and produces wonderful results."*
> —James 5:16 NLT

Abiding in Christ and being submitted to the Word of God is the answer if your desire a powerful prayer life.

> *"But if you remain in me and my words remain in you, you may ask for anything you want, and it will be granted"*
> —John 15:7 NLT

Did you notice you may ask for your desires and they will be granted?

> *"Whatever things you ask when you pray, believe that you receive them, and you WILL HAVE them."*
> —Mark 11:24 NKJ

God wants to give you your heart's desires, but you must delight yourself in God, in His Word, in childlike obedience and total commitment.

> *"Delight yourself in the Lord and he will give you the desires of your heart. Commit your way to the Lord; trust in him and he will do this"*
> —Psalm 37:4, 5 NIV

NOTES

CHAPTER NINE

God wants you to be a winner

The battle is the Lord's but the victory is ours. Jesus has conquered our enemy and given us the authority to enforce this victory.

Winning over temptation

Temptation to sin comes to all and can be very strong, but **it is not a sin to be tempted.** Even Jesus was tempted. God does not take temptation away from you now that you are a Christian. So it is important that you understand how temptation comes, from whom it comes and how to deal with it.

> *"Blessed is the man who endures temptation; for when he has been proved, he will receive the crown of life which the Lord has promised to those who love Him. Let no one say when he is tempted, 'I am tempted by God', for God cannot be tempted by evil, nor does He Himself tempt anyone. But each one is tempted when he is drawn away by his own desires and enticed. Then, when desire has conceived, it gives birth to sin; and sin, when it is full-grown, brings forth death. Do not be deceived, my beloved brethren."*
> —James 1:12-16

God does not tempt you to sin. Satan uses the evil desires that still exist in you to draw you away from God and entice you to sin. Temptation is not sin, but becomes sin when we give in to that evil desire.

You will have many battles with temptation along the road. But each time you win, through the power of the Holy Spirit and your firm stand against sin, it makes you a stronger Christian.

"No temptation has overtaken you except such as is common to man; but God is faithful, who will not allow you to be tempted beyond what you are able, but with the temptation will also make the way of escape, that you may be able to bear it."
—1 Corinthians 10:13

To prevent yourself from sinning, hide God's Word in your heart.

"Your Word I have hidden in my heart, that I might not sin against You."
—Psalm 119:11

Winning over sin through forgiveness

What happens if you are tempted and give in and sin? What should you do?

"If we confess our sins, He is faithful and just to forgive us our sins and to cleanse us from all unrighteousness."
—1 John 1:9

Sin spoils your close relationship with Jesus. If you do something wrong and then just try to forget about it as if nothing had happened you'll find that God will soon seem far away.

You must ..... **stop** ..... **pray** ..... **and confess** what you did wrong to God (fully intending never to do it again); then He will forgive you!

The word 'confess' means to tell God what you did, being very specific, and in no way making excuses for why you did it. For example, if someone said something nasty to you and you replied with something ugly and unkind but later felt sorry, you should NOT confess like this:

"Father, I'm sorry, if I did something wrong there, but you know Mr. A ....was rude to me."

That kind of repentance won't work; it's not real!

This is what you should have said, "Father, I realize I've sinned. I was very unkind and unloving in what I said to Mr. A .... ! Please forgive me."

It is very important that you really try to walk close to God by truly being sorry for any sin you may commit and immediately confessing it without blaming someone else or the circumstances. Always keep a clear conscience.

Resisting The Devil

Satan is our adversary; he wants to steal from you, kill, and destroy you (John 10:10).

One of the main reasons Jesus came to the earth was to destroy the works of Satan and paralyze his power over the human race (1 John 3:8).

Don't be afraid, even though Satan is seeking to destroy you, Jesus will help you if you do your part. You must fight back against the pressures and lies that Satan will try to use on you!

That's right- Fight Back - resist Him! Use the name of Jesus. That's where your authority is.

It's exciting! Something you will soon discover is that living the Christian life God's way - by following Jesus - is the most exciting adventure there could ever be.

"Be sober; be vigilant; because your adversary the devil walks about like a roaring lion, seeking whom he may devour. Resist him, steadfast in the faith..."
—1 Peter 5:8,9

"Therefore submit to God. Resist the devil and he will flee from you."
—James 4:7

One of the ways that you win against the devil is by conquering that sin that is troubling you.

NOTES

_____

_____

_____

_____

_____

_____

_____

_____

_____

_____

_____

_____

_____

_____

_____

_____

_____

_____

_____

_____

_____

_____

_____

CHAPTER TEN

God does not want you to be alone

There will be times in your life when you feel as though God has forsaken you; that your trials and problems are so great, and that you are left on your own to battle through alone. But that is not true; no matter how tough your problem is, **God is with you:**

> *"When you pass through the waters, I WILL BE WITH YOU; and through the rivers, they shall not overflow you. When you walk through the fire, you shall not be burned, nor shall the flame scorch you."*
> —Isaiah 43:2

> *"I WILL NEVER LEAVE YOU nor forsake you."*
> —Hebrews 13:5

> *"Lo, I am with you ALWAYS."*
> —Matthew 28:20

There is a special friendship God has planned for you with Christians; we call it **fellowship.**

When you are enjoying the company of other Christians, something special happens.

*"But if we walk in the light as He is in the light, we have
FELLOWSHIP with one another, and the blood of Jesus Christ His
Son cleanses us from all sin."*
—1 John 1:7

It is wonderful to belong to the Family of God and to meet new
brothers and sisters who really love you! You'll learn to love them too!
This is very important, especially if any of your present friends are a "bad
influence" on you. If they keep pulling you away from serving God by
encouraging you to do wrong things, you will have to start moving away
from them. You will need real Christian friends to "fill the gap." That's
what fellowship is all about. .. learning to share your life with other
Christians and letting them share their lives with you!

Fellowship means:

    a) Sitting **together** over a snack or a meal and talking about what Jesus
       is doing in your life;

    b) **Sharing** gently some new things you have learned in the Bible;

    c) **Praying** for each other;

    d) **Helping** each other around the house, at work, and giving a helping
       hand to get a job done!

    e) Meeting someone's **need** if you can;

    f) Simply being **a friend** you can trust, love and depend on.

Opportunities are many to have fellowship with other Christians.

    a) **Visit** in their homes and invite them to visit you;

    b) **Attend** life group meetings;

    c) **Attend** social or fellowship meetings such as barbecues, picnics,
       family day, etc.

    d) **Invite** the life group you attend around for a pot luck at your home.

NOTES

CHAPTER ELEVEN

God's will is that you be encouraged

AS a born-again believer, it is *very* important that you attend Church **every** Sunday. This is where you have your wounds attended to, receive food for your spirit, a new zeal, and strength to be sent back into the war.

Here are some important reasons why you need to attend church regularly:

1. You will be encouraged and comforted by the Holy Spirit and other believers.

2. You will hear the voice of God speaking to you more clearly at Church than at any other time.

3. You will learn new facts or truths about God and His Word that will help you to live a victorious Christian life.

4. You will enjoy the wonderful privilege of participating in the praise and worship of God.

5. Not only will you be ministered to, but you may even be used by the Holy Spirit to minister to someone else.

"Not forsaking the assembling of ourselves together, as is the manner of some, but exhorting one another, and so much the more as you see the Day approaching."
—Hebrews 10:25

"Now on the first day of the week, when the disciples came together to break bread, Paul, ready to depart the next day, spoke to them and continued his message until midnight."
—Acts 20:7

From now on, you should make a special point of gathering every week with other true Christians to praise and worship God. To do this you'll need to find a NEW TESTAMENT CHURCH to attend.

NOTES

Chapter Twelve

God's will is that you join a New Testament church

There is strength In Unity and Commitment.

Join a New Testament church.

The most important thing you need to do upon being saved and knowing it, is to be added in membership to a local New Testament Church (Acts 2:46,47).

"What is a New Testament Church?" you may ask.

Characteristics of a New Testament church

1. A New Testament Church accepts the headship of the Lord Jesus Christ, which means that the Church is governed or ruled by the Lord Jesus Christ. There are many who say they agree with that, yet reject the final authority of Christ's words if it differs from their personal beliefs or denominational doctrine.

2. A New Testament Church bases its teachings and practices on the Word of God, the Bible. The Bible must be accepted as the supreme and final authority on any issue. The written Word of God never changes nor is subject to our experiences or circumstances.

3. A New Testament Church accepts the Holy Spirit as its guide, teacher, comforter, counselor, helper, advocate, intercessor, strengthener and standby.

4. A New Testament Church has the gifts and power of the Holy Spirit evident and operational. The power of the Holy Spirit is seen when miraculous healings take place, others speak in tongues or interpret these tongues, some people prophesy, and people are being saved. The Church is filled with great joy.

5. A New Testament Church practices the ordinances of water baptism by total immersion and Holy Communion (Covenant Meal).

6. A New Testament Church is filled with joy and excitement because the Kingdom of God is righteousness, peace and joy.

7. In a New Testament Church, the Bible is well taught and the members know Jesus personally as Savior, obey Him as Lord, and are not pew warmers, but enjoy working in the Church.

NOTES

CHAPTER THIRTEEN

God's will is for you to be healed and healthy

There are many benefits and privileges of being in the Kingdom of God. Just to mention a few, you have righteousness, peace, joy; healing, freedom from guilt, condemnation and fear, the power of the Holy Spirit, access to Father God through a powerful prayer life, prosperity, daily forgiveness from sin, etc. Some of these we have already covered, but let's look at a few more.

Healing is provided by God for his children

God wants you well and living in health; that's His plan for you.

> *"Beloved, I pray that you may prosper in all things and be in health, just as your soul prospers."*
> —3 John 1:2

Jesus Himself took your suffering and pain in His body. He purchased healing from all diseases for us. Jesus fulfilled the promise given by the prophet Isaiah...

> *"He Himself took our infirmities (pains, weaknesses) and bore our sicknesses."*
> —Matthew 8:17

It was the whipping of Jesus' body that delivered us from sickness and paid for our healing.

> *"By whose stripes you were healed."*
> —1 Peter 2:24

Thank God He wants you well. Sickness is from the devil. The Holy Spirit anointed Jesus to heal all those who had been made sick by the devil.

> *"How God anointed Jesus of Nazareth with the Holy Spirit and with power, who went about doing good and healing all who were oppressed by the devil, for God was with Him."*
> —Acts 10:38

Sickness does not glorify God, being healed does.

Sickness is not God trying to teach you something, but rather the work of Satan who managed to penetrate your defenses.

SICKNESS IS NOT A BLESSING IN DISGUISE; it comes to kill, steal and destroy. Jesus said: *"The thief does not come except to steal, and to kill, and to destroy. I have come that they may have life, and that they may have it more abundantly."* —John 10:10

That certainly locates Satan's work and God's will. Healing is received by faith.

NOTES

CHAPTER FOURTEEN

God's will for you, his obedient child, is success

God is a success and it should not surprise you that He wants His children to be successful too.

> *"This book of the law shall not depart from your mouth, but you shall meditate in it day and night, that you may observe to do according to all that is written in it. For then YOU WILL MAKE YOUR WAY PROSPEROUS AND THEN YOU WILL HAVE GOOD SUCCESS."*
> —Joshua 1:8

God wants you to be the head and not the tail, i.e., for you to be in charge, in control, giving the orders, being on top of the circumstances and not under them.

> *"The Lord will command the blessing on you in your storehouse (bank accounts), and in all to which you set your hand (work, business) and He will bless you ... And the Lord will make you the head and not the tail, you shall be above only, and not beneath, if you heed the commandments of the Lord your God, which I command you today, and are careful to observe them."*
> —Deuteronomy 28:8,13

It is God's plan and purpose that you as a Christian be successful in life. That you be the head, and not the tail, and that everything to which you apply your hand prospers and succeeds.

NOTES

_____

_____

_____

_____

_____

_____

_____

_____

_____

_____

_____

_____

_____

_____

_____

_____

_____

_____

_____

_____

_____

_____

_____

_____

Chapter Fifteen

God's will is for you to enjoy financial security

Is there life after debt? Yes! Escape from poverty and financial worries, it's God's plan for you.

It is God's revealed, perfect and divine plan for His obedient children to be **free from financial worries.** God has given us a principle to follow to obtain divine prosperity. If obeyed, it would do two things at the same time:

You would have abundance and,

The **Church** would be supported financially to enable it to spread the Good News to others.

God's Principle Is Tithes and Offerings.

The Bible teaches that we should give at least **a tenth** (10%) of our income to God.

> *"For this Melchizedek, king of Salem, priest of the Most High God, who met Abraham ... blessed him, to whom also Abraham gave him a tenth part of all... Now consider how great this man was, to whom even the patriarch Abraham gave a tenth of the spoils."*
> —Hebrews 7:1-4

Disobedience to God's financial requirements will have disastrous financial consequences, while obedience brings divine abundance.

> *"Will a man rob God? Yet you have robbed Me! But you say, 'In what have we robbed you?' In tithes and offerings. You are cursed with a curse, For you have robbed me, even this whole nation.*

Bring all the tithes into the storehouse that there may be food in My house, and prove me now in this, says the Lord of Hosts, if I will not open for you the windows of heaven and pour out for you such a blessing that there will not be room enough to receive it."
—Malachi 3:8-10

This money is to be used to support God's work. **Tithes are to be brought into the local church where you are spiritually** fed. The church is the storehouse where we are fed the bread of life.

In appreciation for our salvation and the sacrifice of Jesus, and in obedience to God's Word, we give our tithe so that others may also be won to Jesus.

Remember, a tithe represents 10/100 or one tenth of **all** your income, but "offerings" is something we give **over and above** our tithe.

Let's look at some of the financial promises for being a faithful giver:

"GIVE, AND IT SHALL BE GIVEN TO YOU: good measure, pressed down, shaken together, and running over will be put into your bosom. For with the same measure that you use, it will be measured back to you."
—Luke 6:38

"He who sows sparingly will also reap sparingly, and he who SOWS BOUNTIFULLY WILL ALSO REAP BOUNTIFULLY. So let each one give as he purposes in his heart, not grudgingly or of necessity; for GOD LOVES A CHEERFUL GIVER. And God is able to make all grace abound toward you, that you always having a sufficiency in all things, have an abundance..."
—2 Corinthians 9: 6-8

Each and every person is expected to give, not grudgingly, but cheerfully. The financial provision is conditional: You must obey and serve God.

"If they obey and serve Him, they shall spend their days in prosperity, and their years in pleasures."
—Job 36:11

God expects you, as a citizen of His Kingdom, to support His Church financially and He promises to bless you financially in return if you do.

(Read '*YOUR RIGHTS TO RICHES*' by Dr. Henry Wolmarans)

NOTES

CHAPTER SIXTEEN

God's will is for you to be free from fear and worry

God offers peace of mind, which is freedom from fear, worry and anxiety. How can I have a sound mind, free from worry? Do what the Bible says:

> *"For God has not given us a spirit of fear, but of power and of love and of a sound mind."*
> —2 Timothy 1:7

> *"Be anxious for nothing, but in everything by prayer and supplication, with thanksgiving, let your requests be made known to God; and the peace of God, which surpasses all understanding will guard your hearts and minds through Christ Jesus."*
> —Philippians 4: 6-7

You must cast your cares on Jesus because He loves you.

> *"Casting all your care upon Him, for He cares for you."*
> —1 Peter 5:7

Why should you worry or fret when the Bible says the very hairs on your head are numbered and not even a sparrow dies without God knowing about it?

NOTES

_____
_____
_____
_____
_____
_____
_____
_____
_____
_____
_____
_____
_____
_____
_____
_____
_____
_____
_____
_____
_____
_____
_____
_____
_____

Chapter Seventeen

There's a miracle in your mouth

The life you will experience tomorrow will be created by your words today.

God wants you to create a bright new and successful future for yourself by **speaking it into being.** Christians have access to a spiritual weapon that unbelievers do not have. It is the ability to speak the Word of God out and HAVE WHATEVER YOU SAY.

> *"For assuredly, I say to you, whoever says to this mountain, 'Be removed and be cast into the sea,' and does not doubt in his heart, but believes that those things he says will come to pass, **HE WILL HAVE WHATEVER HE SAYS."***
> —Mark 11:23

The life you are experiencing today is a direct result of what you said yesterday. You are literally having what you say, good or bad. There is creative power in your words. This is a secret that God has revealed to us, His children.

> *"Death and life are in the POWER OF THE TONGUE."*
> —Proverbs 18:21

If you will control the way you speak and begin to speak positively about your situations, even though they appear bad, your words will change their outcome. You can speak your own future into existence. You can have what you say.

When you speak out God's Word and His promises, believing that they will come to pass, your words become 1,000 times more powerful and productive because God's Word has its own inherent power to produce.

"I am ready to perform My Word."
—Jeremiah 1:12

NOTES

CHAPTER EIGHTEEN

Do you want God's will, God's way, God's power?

God's ultimate goal for you is not heaven; it is for you to be conformed to the image of Jesus.

If you want God's will, God's way and God's power, change is required. You have to do something! Change your thoughts. Renew your mind. This is not merely turning over a new leaf or making a new year's resolution. You must experience an inward change with different thoughts and attitudes which result in different actions.

> *"Let the wicked forsake his way, and the unrighteous man his thoughts; let him return to the Lord, that He may have mercy on him, and to our God, for he will abundantly pardon. 'For My thoughts are not your thoughts, neither are your ways My ways,' says the Lord. 'For as the heavens are higher than the earth, so are My ways higher than your ways and My thoughts higher than your thoughts.'"*
> —Isaiah 55:7-9

The reason our ways are not God's ways is because our thoughts are not God's thoughts, but if we renew our minds, then our thoughts will become God's thoughts and ultimately His ways will become our ways.

> *"Do not be conformed to this world but BE TRANSFORMED BY THE RENEWING OF YOUR MIND, that you may PROVE what is that good and acceptable and perfect WILL OF GOD."*
> —Romans 12:2

We are to be transformed by the renewing of our minds, but

transformed to what? THE IMAGE OF GOD! The question' is: do you desire to change? Is there an internal motivation in you to fulfill God's plan for your life? External laws and restraints will never change you; they will only bring guilt and condemnation. God's ultimate desire, will, plan and purpose for you as a Christian, is not heaven…it is for you to be conformed to the image of Jesus Christ His Son.

"For those whom He foreknew He also predestined to be conformed to the image of His Son, that He might be the first born among many brethren."
—Romans 8:29

This is God's "bull's eye". Don't be discouraged as you aim for it; strive for it and pursue it. God has said that as we have born the image of the earthly man so we must bear the image or the heavenly man (1 Corinthians 15:49). God is at work in you perfecting that which concerns you (Psalm 138:8). You are being transformed into the same image from glory to glory by the Spirit of the Lord (2 Corinthians 3:18) because it's God's plan that you should be as Jesus on the earth (1 John 4:17).

How to Study the Bible

Most believers have probably heard repeatedly how important it is for us to study the Word of God. Yet because many don't understand why, they have a difficult time getting started. So before we get into the how-to of Bible study, let's look at the why-to. Why is studying the Word vital to our Christian growth and maturity?

To understand how vital studying the Word is, we must first understand that the Word of God is alive! The Word can really affect and have a life changing impact on our day-to-day living. God reveals Himself through His Word.

As He reveals Himself to us through His Word, we can expect our lives to change because we are not just getting to know about God, but we are getting to know God Himself! The reason we study the Bible is that we may know God, know His ways and walk in them. Then we can truly live successful Christian lives.

The Bible is a personal message from Almighty God Himself-straight from heaven-to us. The main theme of this message is Jesus-even in the

Old Testament.   Jesus is the living Word, the message of God to all mankind.

Ever since the Fall of Adam in the Garden of Eden, God was unwilling to leave us in our sin and live without us.   So He had a plan-the plan of redemption.   He gave His Son to pay the price for our sin on the cross to bring us back into fellowship with Him, *Glory to God*! So we look for Jesus in every book of the Bible.

All scriptures either point to the Cross or look back on it.   That's why it is so important that we settle in our minds that, while the Bible is God's inspired Word, it is also meant to be down-to-earth.   We are not to just reverently give it a place of honor on our bookshelves, but instead to treat the Word as our personal hands-on reference book on life-a how to book for everyday living.   We must get rid of the negative idea that it is just a set of rules.

God's Word is our very source of liberty.   God sent His Word to set us free, not to bind us up and load us down.   It should to be read with a positive attitude, approaching it as an open door to freedom, not as a list of "do's" and "don'ts."

Now you can begin to see why making the quality decision to set aside time to study the Bible is so important.   We suggest treating this period of study as an appointment that you're required to attend.   Then, every day, follow through by building your schedule around this appointment- and not the other way around.   Soon, you'll develop a desire to attend your study and it will become easier and easier.   And if you miss an appointment once in a while, don't worry; just get back in the flow.

As you get started studying, it is wise to use a Bible you feel free to mark and take notes in.   Start underlining scriptures that have significance and special meaning to you.   This will help personalize the Word for you.   Marking these scriptures will also help you find them more easily when you need them.

At your appointment, one of the best ways to "dig" into the Word is to find a subject or certain scriptures you need to understand, Pray for understanding and discernment of the scriptures.   Allow the Holy Spirit, who inspired the Word of God, to reveal it to you.   Read and think about each word in each scripture.   You can check meanings, too, by using a concordance to study the Greek or Hebrew root words and their meanings.

An important part of your study of the Word is meditation.   To meditate means, "to think deeply and continuously, ponder or reflect."   It also means "to converse with oneself." This takes some time. Read the scripture over and over again as you pray in the spirit. Meditation brings your spirit and your mind together and builds a capacity for your faith to be released (Romans 10:17). Ask the Holy Spirit to open the eyes of your understanding so you can comprehend the deep things of God. Then expect the Lord to do it.

Expect Him to meet you on the level of your need and reveal His Word to you, when starting out, spend the majority of your time in the New Testament (primarily in the letters the Apostle Paul wrote to the early churches). In light of this, we suggest you look for and underline phrases such as "in Him," "in whom" and "in Christ." These phrases are found 134 times in the New Testament from Acts to Revelation, every one of them has something to offer you personally because according to Ephesians 2:6, you are in Christ!

Make what God says the authority in your life. That means you shouldn't just believe what God says to you in His Word, but you should also act on it. Acting on it is what produces results (see Matthew 7:24-27).

Part of acting on the Word includes speaking it. You will find that what you really believe in your heart is what you speak all the time-and what you speak determines what happens in your life (Mark 11:23).

Once you start speaking God's Word about your needs, do not speak anything contrary to it. If you need healing, for example, do not let the focus of your words be about your sickness. Rather confess what the Word says about it: "By His stripes I am healed, according to Isaiah 53:4-5."

Like a sponge, soak in as much Word as possible. Then when you are faced with a situation that requires the wisdom of God, the life of God will flow from you through your words to meet any man's need on any level. And that's the best way to study the Word with the intent of helping and loving others as well as you.

To help in your study, we recommend:

You can also use many different translations of the Bible during your study time. Many study helps and versions of the Bible can be found in almost any local Christian bookstore or online.

Use the books, CDs and DVD's of other ministers but do not allow them to take the place of your personal study time. Take what they have learned and allow the Holy Spirit to add to it. And of course, no matter what material you study, be sure it lines up with God's Word.

Here are some steps to follow in studying the Word:

1. Apply the Word to yourself personally.

2. Allow the Holy Spirit to make the Word a reality in your heart.

3. Carefully ponder how the Word applies to your everyday life.

4. Dwell on how the Word changes your situation.

5. See yourself as God sees you.

6. Realize the integrity of God's Word.

Here is a prayer to pray with confidence as you sit down to study and meditate on His Word:

Father, in the Name of Jesus I come before You today. I take authority over Satan and bind his operation in my life. I pray the eyes of my understanding are enlightened that I may know how rich is Your inheritance in the saints, that I may be filled with the knowledge of Your will in all wisdom and spiritual understanding, walking fully pleasing to You, increasing in the knowledge of You.

Father, I pray I will be rooted and built up in Jesus, established in the faith. I am confident that You who began a good work in me will continue it until the day of Jesus Christ. I know You have heard my prayer, so I know I have the petitions that I asked. Thank You in Jesus' Name.

Prayer References: Ephesians 1:16-18; Colossians 1:9-12,2:6-10; Philippians 1:6; 1 John 5:14-15.

NOTES

Made in the USA
San Bernardino, CA
30 July 2019